I AM MY OWN DAD

When Your Children Mean So Much

Paul Posey Sr.

A'Lure Publishing LLC

I Am My Own Dad, Unloved, and When You Wake Up

Copyright © 2023, 2016

Paul Posey Sr.

The Book Cover and Title Page were designed by Paul A. Posey.

Contact Me

For information, contact:

www.alurepublishllc.com

info@alurepublishing.com

www.facebook.com/N2PInc

Instagram: Neg_2_Pos

Twitter: mrneg2pos

I'm available for public speaking, motivational events, and family workshops. To schedule a date, contact me at: http://www.n2pga.org/contact-us.html

I AM MY OWN DAD

When Your Children Mean So Much

Bonus Books:

Unloved

When You Wake Up

Three In One Book

I Am My Own Dad
When Your Children Mean So Much

Unloved
The Residue Of Dysfunction

When You Wake Up
Let The Healing Begin

I AM MY OWN DAD

TABLE OF CONTENTS

PREFACE

I want to share why I felt it was necessary to be my own dad. As human beings, we are born with the ability to generate change and find ways to improve our lives, circumstances, and situations. When a young man has no dad, there are neither guidelines nor a base from which to mold himself. Quite often, they are forced to "wing it" and go through a lot of trials and tribulations that sometimes yield lifelong scars. These scars can descend on their children and their children's children.

In this reading, I will take you on a journey through the eyes and ears of a boy who had no dad and no choice. It is not my goal to bash the moms out there but to give an insight into what a boy with missing pieces goes through emotionally to survive and be a great dad to his children.

If you have a young man who does not have a role model—a granddad, uncle, or neighborhood dad—who is not afraid to share his dad's skills, please connect him with one.

My Disclaimer:

I am no scholar; I don't have a degree in child psychology. I am a boy who wanted a dad, so I made one out of myself.

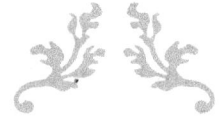

MISSING PIECES

Growing up, I was the third of five children. My sister is the oldest, followed by a brother and a set of twins who were born four years after me. My sister had a dad; we would see him when it was her birthday. He would bring her gifts, and she was semi-connected to his family. My older brother visited his dad a few times, and I was forced to tag along for their visits. His dad later died, which kind of left my brother in the same boat as I was, but at least he had a chance to meet his father. The father of the twins was in our lives for a few years, but it was clear to me that he was not my dad, and attempting to connect with his family was a constant struggle.

It took me several years to realize that I had no dad. I watched my siblings have moments of pride and sadness with their dads. I gave hugs to those I did not belong to and knew deep down inside that I was not a part of their family. At approximately ten years old, I started asking, "What about me?" My mother told me my father was dead. She shared no pictures or stories of their marriage, how they met and fell in love, or about the wonderful child they created. There was no mention of grandparents, aunts, or cousins that I could contact to find out anything about my father. It was her goal not to allow him to exist in my life. As I recall, no one in my extended family said anything about him either. All I could do was daydream about what it would be like to have a dad of my own.

Do not get it twisted; I had two mountains in my life that I looked up to as models of manhood. First is my grandfather, a man of few words, a great work ethic, and world-class problem-solving skills. It was not his overt intent to teach me what I should do as a man; I just paid attention to how he handled our family and how he was well-respected in the community. Second was Mr. Johnson; he was an elderly neighbor who always sat on his porch and made himself visible to the kids. We would ask him questions, and he'd answer them, and he always gave good advice. Even as an adult, I would still go to the old block just to sit and talk with him and let him know that his presence meant the world to me.

PAIN AND ANGER

As I see it, people are made up of ingredients—ingredients that make us "whole people." When people are not whole, they constantly search for the missing pieces without even knowing that they are missing at all. When there are open holes in a person, we tend to fill them with pain and anger. In my case, it became a silent suffering, where I would cry alone when my siblings weren't around, always asking, "What about me?" The pain of the realization that my father had been erased from the family story was heartbreaking.

My pain turned to anger—a deep, hidden anger that could not be doused by sharing my sister's or brother's dad. I was angry at my dad, angry that he left me. I know it sounds crazy to be angry with a man I had never set eyes on before, a man who never sat me on his knee, made me laugh, or wiped one tear. That anger grew and grew, which, as I see it today, often spewed out as rage. That rage was like a battery inside of me that I could tap into if I were in danger or in a fight to save my life.

I Am My Own Dad

When I see the young men of today, I see that same look in their eyes. I see that little boy asking, "What about me?" as they walk down the middle of the street, daring oncoming cars to strike them down. I see the same pain and anger I felt as a child with missing pieces. They have a hidden pain they cannot verbalize. Even worse, they have anger, and that anger can be expressed in an extremely negative way that can hurt them for the rest of their lives.

FATHERS AND MOTHERS

They are builders, providers, teachers, doctors, and ultimately our first loves. When you have an absent parent, the odds against the child becoming a whole person become greater. Fathers and mothers play key roles in raising children. Their involvement goes way beyond their biological makeup. Yes, they will get their height, smile, and hair from their parents. But the ingredients that make them good friends and loving partners in relationships come from their fathers and mothers.

When those ingredients are not provided by the father and mother, the children seek out the missing pieces in others. This is where the extended family must step in, i.e., grandparents, aunts, uncles, cousins, and stepparents. Extended family members do not replace the yearning for the love and lessons to come from a child's very own father and mother.

Mothers who are forced to provide the ingredients for their children without the help of their fathers tend to face many challenges. They often take on the roles of father and mother for their children. She must be the nurturer and the disciplinarian at the same time, which twists her as well as the child. Sometimes the nurturer loses out to the disciplinarian, and vice versa. She suffers from being torn between both jobs. She deals with protecting and providing at the same time as well. This is a very difficult position to be in, and quite often, help does not come.

Fathers who had no father or positive role model to follow when growing up are at a loss. They have no clue what their roles are or how their absence affects their children. They are often still yearning for their missing pieces themselves. Without consciousness of their position, they are bound to repeat the same cycle for their children. In my opinion, fathers have the most important role. Fathers must lead their children, not control them or own them, but model the abilities they want their children to have as adults. Fathers should be in tune with the child's mother and decide what their parenting goals are for their children. When no one knows their role and the right ingredients are not given to the child, then the angry world will fill the child up. Once a child is filled with the feeling of being **unloved**, it can lead them down a path of pain. It often takes years for a child to get grounded and get their life on track. Also, it is paramount that your children are conscious of the roles of parents before they become fathers and mothers.

MEETING MY DAD

Remember when I said my mom said my dad was dead? Well, I came to find out he was not dead at all. Let me tell you the story.

One day, while my wife was at a gas station back in my hometown of Gary, Indiana, she was driving a car with my last name on the front bumper plate. A man comes up and asks her, "Which part of the Posey family are you?" Through conversation, she finds out that this man was my dad. At the time, I was a Staff Sergeant stationed in Washington State, serving in the United States Marine Corps. She called me with him standing right there, and I spoke to him for the first time. Of course, this raised a thousand and one questions I wanted to ask but did not. I was scared and thrilled at the same time. I quickly planned to go to him. My dad gave me some information about his other children. I came to find out that I was the eldest of his kids; there were three other boys and one girl, the same number of children that my mom had. He told me that my brother closest to me was living in

Gary, which happened to be one block down from my grandfather's house.

I made it to my hometown a few days later. As I was traveling to my grandfather's house, I remembered the address of the house where my brother was living. It turned out to be my aunt's old home, where I used to play as a child. You could have knocked me down with a feather. I was supposed to meet my dad the next day, but I couldn't help but visit my brother down the street that afternoon. I went to my grandfather's house and told him what was going on. I can't quite remember his response to the whole thing. I left his home and walked down the street to the house. I rang the doorbell, and a young man answered the door. I introduced myself: "I'm Paul Posey, and I was told I am your older brother." He told me his name was James Posey, the same as my dad's. He said, "I'm not sure what to say, but my mother is here; you have to talk with her." His mom came from behind the door and said, "I heard about you, but I thought you were just a rumor. What am I supposed to say to a twenty-seven-year-old son?" I kindly told her, "Let's try saying hello. I am not here to haggle over my mom and dad's relationship and the lies he may have told, but I'm here to meet my brother." That pretty much put things on the table. Now that I had a new brother, it was time to meet my dad and the others.

One of the scariest things in the world is coming face-to-face with something you have dreamed about most of your life. There were no stories or pictures to measure who I was about to meet.

I drove to his house, but he was not there. My new brother was there with the other two younger brothers, a sister, and their mom. The boys were thrilled to meet me, and I was happy to meet them as well. My sister gave me a look of disgust and did not say a word to me. My dad's wife was a lot warmer and more respectful to her new twenty-seven-year-old son. I answered questions and asked questions about them while waiting to meet my dad. I was told he was at work at the time, but it wasn't too far from the house. I couldn't wait any longer, so I asked my brother to show me where his job was. It was a short drive to his job; he worked at a buy-here, pay-here car lot.

My dad was about 5'9" tall and about 225–240 lbs. He still had all his hair, which I thought was pretty cool. His belly was round and sticking out a bit, like a beer-belly starter kit. He had the smile of a chocolate-colored Halloween pumpkin, with his missing teeth. He had a nervous laugh about him, the kind that comes with uncertainty. I was uncertain too, but there we were, finally face-to-face.

We had a nice, cordial conversation, yet we spoke very little of Mom. I shared information about my career in the Marines and the places I had been. We talked about my wife and where we lived in the city before we moved to Washington. We laughed about how he and my wife met at a gas station. It was a glorious but short meeting because he was at work. I told him I would come back the next afternoon with my children to meet their grandfather.

Right then, I felt a calmness come over me. The fire of being unwanted, unloved, and yearning for my dad went out. I was not looking for him to answer a lot of questions about who, what, when, and why. I had met my dad, and I was about to add another chapter to my life.

So I thought...

MEET MY MOM

I know, why would a man leave his son and let him think he was dead all those years? From my understanding, there is a backstory to my tale, which was coated with pain and anger. This pain belonged to my mother. Only a woman hurt so badly would wish a man to be dead and then let her son think the same.

My mom wanted to be forever young; she told us to call her Tina. Mother, mom, and momma were not to be in our vocabulary. Tina was a steelworker, and no matter what, she always found a way to make it work. As far back as I can remember, my mom was a fighter. She never backed down from an argument, and she never surrendered in a fight. She cursed as if she had made the words up herself. My mom was such a beautiful Tasmanian devil that once she got started, we knew we were doomed and prayed for sleep. She stood about 5'4", maybe 130 lbs. I often thought if ass whooping were in the Olympics, she would take the gold in the one- and two-hand beatdowns. She whooped us everywhere she found us: at school, baseball practice, down the block, at the store, in the alley behind the house, basically anywhere she found us. She was not shy about it; she even whooped us in other people's houses.

She organized us like little soldiers, and we functioned as a team, caring for the house. All the chores were on the fridge, organized by day and person. We shoveled the snow, raked the leaves, cut the grass, and did laundry, including ironing our clothes. Most would think it was admirable to have your children in tune like a well-oiled machine. However, my mother's parental strategy lacked the one-on-one love and compassion every child should receive. These were my earliest recollections of our lives, from ages eleven down to five at the time.

What I need to share about my mother is that she was a functional alcoholic, and her drink of choice was Wild Irish Rose. The more she drank, the meaner she got. She fought like a prizefighter with those she deemed she loved. The men in her life loved and feared her because she was as volatile as gasoline at a barbeque; sure, you can get things started, but it can quickly get out of hand. I've seen her beaten to the ground and cried myself to sleep, wishing I could have saved her. I used to pity my mother for what I saw her go through.

As I got older, I came to understand that my mom was not always the victim but more like a bully at times. My extended family feared my mom, and she seemed to be proud of it. She didn't have loving relationships with her siblings. She didn't like to speak about her childhood, and to ask too many questions about it would be asking to feel her bite.

It was hard to express how I felt about not seeing my dad like the rest of the kids. She was very closed-mouthed. Still, today, I do not know the truth about why he was not a part of my life. There were a few times I felt a need to talk with her about my dad, their marriage, their separation, and my separation from my wife. The conversation went like this:

Conversation #1

Me: "Me and Bree are going to separate."

Mom: "Oh really?"

Me: "But I'm not going to do like my dad did me."

Mom: "What do you mean?"

Me: "I'm going to see my kids, not like he did me; he never came to see me."

Mom: "He didn't see your motherf*%ing ass because I didn't want him to."

Mc: (Silent tears)

This second conversation with Tina took place when I called to tell her I had found my dad.

Conversation #2

Me: "Guess what?!"

Mom: "What?"

Me: "Bree found my dad!"

Mom: "Where?"

Me: "She ran into him at a gas station."

Mom: "Oh well."

Me: "Why did you tell me he was dead?"

Mom: "He was dead to me."

Me: "Why didn't you tell me he was alive, right in the same town? Did you know?"

Mom: Yeah, I knew; I saw him at the grocery store after you left for the Marines.

Me: "… Why didn't you tell me, like when I was ten or thirteen, to let me decide? **What about me?!**"

Mom: "What the f*%& about you?"

Me: "… Never mind, bye."

"Hurt people, hurt people." N2P

It was at this moment that I knew I did not know her. I mean, who in the world would give such a cold and mean response to a child they birthed? My mother's hatred has no limit, through time or people.

LEAVING MY DAD

I thought this was the beginning of a new era in my life, meeting my dad, his wife, three brothers, and an angry sister. Everything I dreamed about was coming true. The pain that I endured watching my siblings with their dads was going to fade away. The whole trip from Washington to Indiana, I was cheering myself on, smiling, and making plans to infiltrate my new family. I felt brand new, thinking my children were going to have a grandfather and grandmother to create lifelong experiences with.

I woke up the next morning with my wife and kids. We took special care to make sure my two daughters were looking brand new, and my son was still a baby. I called my dad to confirm the time I was to get there. I told him I would bring lunch for everyone; KFC is always great for impromptu family reunions. My wife had to work, so it was just the children and me. I had called before I got to the house, just to make sure, because I didn't want anything to ruin the moment, and I had everything important to me in that car.

When we got there, my dad and two of the boys were on the front porch. We waved and smiled from the car. I gathered the kids and the food and cut across the yard to the house. As I approached the porch, the strong smell of weed, marijuana, reefer, or whatever you want to call it, hit my nose. I asked my dad if he had been smoking weed. He said, "Aww, me and the boys were just fooling around a bit with it." I was crushed yet again by someone who I thought gave a damn about me. This was an even worse feeling because I brought my future and my children to meet him. The only thing I could say was, "Kids, say hello and goodbye to your granddaddy; this will be the last time you see him."

Pain and anger—now let's add humiliation and disgust. Who in their right mind greets their unknown grandchildren smelling like a street clown? I did everything I could not to show my dad what I learned in the Marines. How dare you embarrass my special moment in life by "just fooling around?" Where in the handbook of bringing a divided family together after twenty-six years does smoking weed come in?

I stayed true to my word; I broke bread with my new family, and I shared my hopes and dreams of what I wanted for my children, and then I left. My dad never saw my children again. I knew in my mind that I was not going to have a relationship with my dad; he stole a precious moment from me, which I find unforgivable. He also did not get to know how great I was before he met me or the kind of dad I was to my children.

My dad just became dead to me.

MODELED
BEHAVIOR

"When you make dysfunction the norm to your children, it becomes their norm." N2P

We, as children, emulate what we see. I remember that from time to time, my older brother and I would dress in my mom's steel millwork boots and helmet and make impressions of her. My mom was more of a dad for most of our lives. Like when we were eleven and ten, she let us drive the car. Well, she was drunk one night and called home from the bar and told us to get the keys to the car and drive to get her, and that is exactly what we did. We got in the car, and we talked our way to starting and driving more than ten blocks to her favorite watering hole. It was fun for us; we laughed, and to our surprise, we drove the car without hitting anything. We had watched her drive; we also knew the direction of the flow of traffic and the use of turn signals. However, parking was not our forte that night. We double-parked

19

the 1970-something Chevy Impala just outside the bar. After giving each other a high five for making that journey, we had to go inside to get my mom. We went inside the bar; it was smoky, and people were laughing and screaming. We weren't sure if we could find her. About two feet in, a man asked us, "What do you two want?" I said, "We are here to pick up our mom; her name is Tina." The man told us to wait outside, and he would get her. A few minutes passed, and she came to the door. She was with a few smelly friends, and she bragged to them how we drove the car from home to the bar to get her. We felt pretty good, but all of that was so wrong.

There are pluses for young boys to have a mom who can work like a man, drink like a man, and, from time to time, fight like a man. I learned a lot from Tina, like how to drive and how important it is to go to work. She also did a "Don King," where she promoted my first fight with the bully down the street. I was proud of her strength and her tenacity. Tina was a first-class cusser; she cussed us so much that we thought "mother%@er" was our given name. It really helped when I joined the Marines. I shoveled out the f-bomb like I had been in the service for ten years. Those were things we definitely knew about Tina.

What we did not know then was that Tina was a functional alcoholic. She was mad at the world, and many felt her wrath. I had spent many of my adult years trying to have some heartfelt conversations with Tina to gain insight into her childhood. Who did she play with? What were our grandparents like when she was a child? Her life was a mystery, and she buried the good and the bad of her childhood in a bottle. There was only one picture of Tina when she was a child. The only other picture of her was in a high school classroom as a student. Funny, there were no pictures of me as a baby, and I only remember taking a few pictures as a child outside of school picture day.

Let's tally up my role models thus far. We have my mom, dad, grandfather, and Mr. Johnson. They were all pretty consistent in my life from age ten until I married and started having my own children.

My grandfather lost his wife when I was nine. I loved her like the sun, and I missed her twice as much when she passed away. My grandmother was the softest thing I had in my life. Her death loosened the glue in our whole family. I stuck to my grandfather as close as I could because I knew he missed her, and he was my second-greatest love. I would spend the weekends with him; it didn't matter how short the time was, I wanted to be with him. By this time, he was no longer working at the steel mill. He was a security guard and helper at the local liquor store two blocks from our house. I'd even ride my bike down the street just to see his car outside his job. Everyone respected my grandfather; I don't think that the 357 Magnum he had on his side had much to do with it.

I also had Mr. Johnson right down the street to occasionally talk about current events and life. He worked in the mill like my mom, but I'm sure they were on different shifts. His simple attention to what we were doing on the block made me feel safe. He had his sons; they were much older than me. I watched him interact with them; he'd give them directions and things to do. I never saw him being mean to them, at least from what I could see. His boys were people I used to look up to, and they never treated the smaller kids badly.

These are the people from whom I extracted the fundamentals of who I was going to be as a man.

BREAKING THE CYCLE

A woman once told me, "I'd rather have a bad dad than no dad at all." This statement struck home for me. By this time, I was a father of five and well on my way to repeating the cycle of not living up to my role as a dad. I was an inside dad, an outside dad, and an absent dad all at the same time. At this point in my life, I was "winging it." To me, I was winging my way through life and taking everyone with me. I had little idea of the direction I wanted to take my children. With not having a dad, I did not have to go from a negative place of parenting, i.e., dealing with abuse or a drunken dad. I had no dad, which put me in a neutral position about the type of dad I would be.

People don't think; we tend to live by way of emotional decisions, and those decisions are often based on feeling good as soon as possible, which often comes back and bites us in the ass of life. Poor decision-making when it comes to our children can create a generational curse that can very well affect their children as well. I did not want my children to be dysfunctional and learn life's lessons from broken people with broken ways. They could end up being connected to bad friends trying to teach them costly shortcuts to life based on instant gratification. I had to generate a list of must-haves for being a great dad.

MAKING OF A DAD

There are moments in life when you must make up your mind about how your children will grow. When it comes to being a dad, it is the most important decision you can make for generations to come. This role requires your ability to accept another dad's wisdom, be your child's role model, have money to take care of your family, have patience, fear, blind trust, a hint of rage, and the willingness to sacrifice your today for your child's tomorrow. Notice I did not say love. Love is the reason you do everything. However, that love starts with you wanting them to have the best possible chance at a great life. But more often than not, you want them to have it better than you did.

So, let's break it down:

"The ability to accept another dad's wisdom" has proven to be extremely hard yet most useful. Wisdom is a life lesson layered with pain. When wisdom is handed down, it is called knowledge—the knowledge that was previously paid for by the loss of life, money, and tears of those before you. People share wisdom because they do not wish to see others go through the very same thing they went through. Wisdom is often given away freely in conversation. People post it on social media as memes, jokes, and even videos. I often say, "You can learn a lot from a dummy." A dummy is not a dumb person, as negative-minded people quickly assume. Everyone you see and hear can be your dummy, as it has been coined in the Ad Council commercials on safety belts. A man's lack of wisdom and knowledge of his role as a dad is not an excuse. However, it could scar those who are in his charge, from mothers to children, nieces, and nephews, and you can add stepchildren as well.

"Be your child's role model." Whatever fundamentals you want your child to have, you must model and teach them. If you want your child to be an advocate for the weak, you must champion for the weak yourself. Being a parent is not based on telling children what you want them to do. You **must** show them through action. Dads and moms are the primary teachers, and what you do in front of children, they will do. Some will argue this because they are looking at the negative things their children have done but forget to look at the good things they do as well.

If you do not model for your child, they will get their lessons elsewhere. We tend to forget that a child is a sponge, and they mimic what they see daily, especially when you don't take notice. They are always paying direct attention. A great example is swearing or cussing.

My mom cussed so much that I use it in my daily conversation. She would use cuss words in an angry and condescending way. Now I use cuss words in regular situational conversation to drive a point home, minus the negative meanings. Thanks, Tina.

You cannot expect children to emotionally connect to your old pains and tribulations that you went through as a child. The lack of **"money"** that you had to endure as a child should not be their legacy. This also means you should engage in legitimate employment to support your children, or at the very least try. You lose all rights to "wing it" with your child's life. Thoughts of being a dope man, cigarette hustler, or booster as a source of employment are for single-minded people. Any job that solely rests on you not getting caught is not a good gamble for your child. I'm not saying it cannot be done, but if you were arrested for illegal activity, your children could very well not eat. At some point, you must have a plan, and that plan should create a legacy for your children. Selfish plans yield selfish results, which can leave your children out in the cold.

Rome was not built or designed in a day. Applying a large dose of **"patience"** helps when it comes to teaching and modeling for your children. It is not a one-time deal where you share it and forget it. If you are teaching your son how to change a tire, do not show him once; find ways to practice that skill. Calling AAA is not teaching your son a skill. Teaching him what tools are needed, where to stage the car, the right location of a jack, and how to create a safe condition to do the work is giving him a skill. That gives your child confidence in what you have taught them.

Dads need to have a **"fear"** of failing their children. We live in a world where any little slip-up can land someone in jail or a grave. Teach them skills to reduce the fear that we have each time they leave our sight. Parents who get high with their children have no fear. They do not care how their child turns out. Fear is not your enemy; it is a state of mind where you do not want the negative outcome of life's situations to happen to your children. I had no immediate fear for years until my grandsons were born. I did not know what type of dads would be in their lives. That is the fear of the unknown, and their tomorrow means so much to me. To conquer this fear, I can only stay ready to model and teach them the skills and life lessons that are greater than me.

"Blind Trust" is when you allow your child to venture out into the world to utilize the skills you have taught them. You cannot micromanage your child's walk because they will never find self-confidence in their skills and decision-making. You should trust that what you have modeled and taught them will kick in like a second sense. They are humans. They will fail you from time to time, but without your wisdom, it will be hard to turn things in the right direction. We were all children before; we know the traps out there. Accepting the traps as a part of life or the norm is foolish, especially if you know the historical outcome. So, you must teach the traps as well as the fundamentals.

Paul Posey

"A hint of rage" creates a call to action to teach the urgency of a lesson, like a mother grizzly bear protecting her cubs or creating a mental footprint in your child's mind like a Drill Instructor in Marine Corps Boot Camp. We know the world and the people in it don't care much about the next person. They truly do not value your children as much as you do. You must be willing to step into the lion's den and be ready for combat. I once made no bones about how I was capable of breaking the arm of my daughter's wannabe boyfriend. He gained some fear from my rage, and we had a clear and mutual understanding.

"The willingness to sacrifice your today for your child's tomorrow" simply means that you must stay in character as a parent to ensure your child launches with skills and functional knowledge of how to conduct themselves out in the world. When you put all those things in play, from accepting wisdom to a hint of rage, your plate is full. There is no time to club like you did in your twenties. There is no time to do drugs or fist-fight your partner. You are your child's cardinal teacher, and you are in charge of their tomorrow. There is no such thing as "They will learn as I learned" or "You need yours; I got mine." Those are the statements of a hurt person who cannot muster up enough self-love to give love to a child. Whatever you wanted to do as an adult before you started having children should be put on hold. I'm not saying you cannot plan your empty nester years; by all means, plan what you are going to do with their rooms after they move out. However, from their birth to the day they launch, the class is in session, and you are

the primary teacher.

I'll never hear, "You never taught me anything."
That is the battle cry of a hurt child who must learn life
lessons while on the streets.

PICKING UP THE PIECES

It took a divorce and several years to earn my children's respect. All those things I shared earlier were my guidelines for reinventing my role as a dad. There were nights I cried because the love I thought I deserved was being directed toward their mothers, but I stayed the course. I did not live by those negative statements that rang through my ears as a child. My children had no clue what I went through as a child until the writing of this book. Even though I too fell into the cycle of dysfunction, I had to come up with something to guide me through the process.

SIX STEPS TO GETTING BACK ON TRACK

Love them and love yourself. Loving yourself is crucial; without love for oneself, it is hard to project love onto

31

others. Find ways to show love to your children besides money and gifts. It is going to hurt, but it is well worth it to gain their respect and feel their love.

Tell the truth. When your child asks a question, always answer with the unfiltered truth; they have already heard the lies and the other side of the story. Do not say anything you cannot take back or undo. You might want to do more listening than talking.

Accept their responses. Whatever they say to you will probably come from a place of pain. You cannot argue with a person's opinion or emotion. Lashing out, crying, and some cussing may occur in the beginning. It just has to run its course. Remember, the pain of rejection and loss has been sitting with them for years; it may take an undisclosed amount of time to establish a meaningful relationship.

Show that you are human. If you feel like crying, hugging, or sharing, it's all part of life. This is no place for pride or trying to protect your feelings. Tell them how much you miss them, too. It is helpful to show how you feel—good, bad, or indifferent.

Keep your word. The worst parenting, or lack thereof, comes from letting your child down by way of lies and false commitments. Your word will be the new standard, and everything you say can and will be held against you.

Get ready to model. Your children are going to want lovable grandparents for their children; therefore, get your life together. You still have value in their lives; show it.

FROM FATHER TO DAD

I watch fathers every day; they come home from work, pull into the garage, and go into the house. The blinds are drawn all day, every day. There is no village if all the villagers are hiding in their homes and the children are out on the streets. I see the neighborhood children because I am the Mr. Johnson of my block. I make myself visible to help fix bikes and cars and answer questions they may have. I'm keeping my skills sharp for my grandsons by being Mr. Johnson. Father is a title; a dad is a role that must be displayed. Being a dad is a full-time job; it automatically kicks in around children. There are times you have to make your presence known even more to let them know you care.

I cried a few times while writing this book, reliving the pain that I have been carrying for years. None of my friends from childhood knew my pain. There is no strength in storing pain; the true strength is in letting it go. People will always tell you that "We all have to go through some things in life." In my world, that is a lie; I didn't need to go through life without a dad. I did not want my children to go through it either. They are loved, and I teach them things I learned every chance I get. I want them to be in the business of making better Poseys.

If you are a man who has no dad, do as I did; make your own dad in you. Children need dads, and moms need partners in raising their children. It is not for you; it is for them. If you have failed a child, by all means, try to fix it, because they will be parents one day too, and the cycle of dysfunction must stop to make a better tomorrow.

BONUS BOOK 1

UNLOVED

The Residue of Dysfunction

TABLE OF CONTENTS

PREFACE

Watching the news and reading about the violence in the streets, you cannot miss the bottom-line issue that is destroying our tomorrow. Our youth are in pain, and the violence we see is a cry for help. The senseless killings and actions are symptoms of a bigger issue called family dysfunction. The looks these young men give strangers are heartbreaking. They are ready for death every morning when they wake up. However, for me, it is more than just a simple observation. It was a familiar pain that I had buried so deeply that it forced me to disconnect and block many things from my past. I do not like my old pain, but I would gladly meet that pain again to stop the storm of pain that is plaguing our youth today. So help me, God.

I SEE YOU

I see you through my dad's filter and as a member of the community, and I feel your pain. While carrying out my daily duties of housing homeless veterans, I see our young people in apartment complexes, places of employment, or just walking through the communities. Some look uncared for and emotionally numb. I personally want to say I'm sorry from the bottom of my heart that you must endure this unnecessary pain.

It is hard for me to tell children that I understand their hurt and emotional neglect without sharing my personal pain. There are many parents out there who have suffered similar pain. Most of us stand tall and push the pain deep inside in order to make life look easy to our children. You would be surprised at the number of adults who have been where you are. We hide our scars very well. There are a few of us who hurt so badly that we are propelled to be a part of the solution—bringing healing to our broken children.

To get things on track, it will take a village to embrace you and douse the pain that has been handed down from your parents and, most likely, their parents.

THE HOUSE OF PAIN

I will take you on a journey to share what I mean by "unloved." Unloved is a feeling that some of the children have, no matter what the household dynamics are. It is the numbing of joy and hope. It is a lack of feeling that turns good kids into bad ones. If not corrected, it turns into a family poison called dysfunction.

I was born and raised in Gary, Indiana, at Mercy Hospital, a stone's throw away from the United States Steel Corps. My mother was a steel worker there; she worked in what they called the Coke Plant. From what I could see from the front gate, it was a harsh place to work. I watched the steel mill's salaries hold families together and douse the flame of a family with their demands on their workers' time.

I am one of the five children my mother had. Being the middle child, I was able to see what not to do and what to avoid. I have an older sister and brother who were born a year apart. After me are my two young brothers, who are twins. My mom had a great-paying job. We lived in a nice neighborhood right down the road from the mill. For those who know of Gary, IN, we lived on 6th and Buchanan St. That was right in the middle of the two major hospitals, Methodist Hospital and Mercy Hospital. Back then, we did the things that other families did. We had picnics; we went to city events, parades, and festivals. One time, I remember seeing Richard Gordon Hatcher on a float in a parade. Back then, I thought all mayors were black; I didn't know he was making history. Our schools were within walking distance, and we would walk to and from school in groups. Everything seemed normal back then. We were latchkey kids, and we followed most of the rules. We did our best not to get caught.

My mother was not your normal mother. As children, we used to call her by her first name. She smoked and drank regularly. From time to time, she would have friends over to the house. They would drink and play cards. My mother had two modes: extremely happy and extremely mad. When she was mad, we all knew what was coming. I'm not saying we were angels; we tried to be normal kids. She ruled us with a swift hand and harsh words. My mother systematically kept us in line. She wrote out our chores and pasted them on the refrigerator. The year was about 1976 or 77. I can say those were the best years I could remember as a family unit. As far as I knew, that was when the word dysfunction was invented.

I can remember as clear as day when our world changed. My mother came home one day and told us that she had gotten married. Yes, just like that—no warning, no wedding. We did not know she was even dating him. My mother had married someone she knew from years ago and just brought him home. If the devil had a child on earth, it was him. He stood about 5'6" with a slim to medium build. He had a receding hairline where you could see the veins at the temples of his forehead. He had extremely large eyeballs; they looked like they could barely fit in the eye sockets. His hands seemed black on both sides and looked like he ate nails for dessert, chewing them down to the nub. He had the worst set of teeth I had ever seen, and we stared into his mouth every time he spoke. We were in for an ugly treat, and our lives would never be the same.

He seemed to hate us coming through the door. We could do nothing right in his eyes, and it seemed to me that my mother had no clue as to what was going on. I almost felt like she brought him home just to terrorize us. During this period of our lives, my mom was a functioning alcoholic—another new word I learned. She and her husband would fight as if they were UFC fighters, and the title match was held in the living room weekly.

This guy was a piece of work. He was a habitual liar and lied about everything to everyone, including our neighbors, our baseball coaches, and even the reverend down the street. He was a thief and a bit of a thug. He was so bad; once he stole my brother's paper route money and blamed it on me. Funny, before he moved in with us, there was no thievery in the house. He began to steal money from my mother's purse, bank account, and even her Bible. Between my mother and him, they wrecked every car she had until they split. Later, we found out that he was a cokehead, which was another new term we learned back then.

Unloved was my older brother; her husband would torment him the most out of the five of us. It hurt me to watch my brother receive the brunt of her husband's rage. Unloved is how he would disgrace our family in front of our neighbors. Unloved is watching my mother become so powerless that she could not and would not protect us from him. Unloved is how she stayed with him after his antics caused us to move from house to house because the rent and mortgage money went up his nose. Unloved is not letting anyone save us.

By 1983, it was the norm to witness the beatings of my siblings, my mother's loss, and stolen wages, and to be forced to watch her get beaten to a bloody pulp at times. She kept us in that hell, and I cannot and will not try to imagine what was going through her head.

We finally got rid of him. We had moved into a little house down by the railroad tracks on the west side of Gary. On this day, we had planned to take a stand. This would be the first time we pooled together to take back our family. By this time, my brother and I were barely big enough to make one man. Our godbrother was there for support, just in case another fight took place. I was chosen as the spokesperson for the kids. With two hairs on my chest, I told the devil, "We have no more room; we cannot move into anything smaller than where we are; you have to go." My mother stood there and had no words for him or us. We all stood in the kitchen for a few seconds in silence. He told my mother to take him to his mother's house, which was way on the east side of Gary. We knew what that meant—he was going to beat her again. This time I said, "We're all going," and that's what we did. My godbrother, my older brother, and I got into the car with them. It was a long, quiet ride across town; we made it without incident. We dropped the gargoyle off at his mother's house, and we did not see him for years until I was well into my career with the Marine Corps.

THE
DYSFUNCTIONAL
FIVE

This was only a battle in the war of dysfunction. My mother's choice of who she married had long-term consequences for us as children. I could not fathom why my mother was so cold and neglected our need for love. The scars of not being connected to her have affected all five of us. We never had the ability to love and have a healthy relationship. We never silicified through bonding with my mother.

We did not know we were dysfunctional or how my mom's marriage would affect our pursuit of relationships. We attempted to move on with our lives, not knowing we needed healing from our ordeal. Our relationship compass was extremely off, and we made a lot of bad choices about who we loved. By 1984, we had started having kids. First, my sister, then me, followed my brother James. I think it might be safe to say that sex was the self-prescribed medication for dysfunction. We hurt so badly and craved love that we tended to substitute sex for the missing love of a parent. If you do this, you open your future to a lot of pain. This pain is not just for the injured; it can spill into the lives of your children as well.

For years, we all went our separate ways; we were not as tight as we used to be. My older brother was the first to make his journey outside the state of Indiana. I followed my goal of being a Marine; I even left home three months early. My twin brothers dropped out of school, and their map to a successful launch was shredded. My mom continued to drink, and she had pretty much given up on parenting them, and they had to fend for themselves. I do not remember us talking as a group about what happened during those years.

"The words of a mother and father can be the greatest and most powerful thing you ever hear or the worst sounds that could ever pass through a child's ears." N2P

THE HOLLOW PEOPLE

By 2011, all the boys had been married and divorced. My sister was not married, which made us pretty even across the board. No one could sustain a healthy relationship. I single-handedly ruined my marriage by subconsciously seeking the love of a mother instead of paying attention to my wife. By the time of my divorce, I had started waking up from the spell of dysfunction. I could not undo what had been done. All the things I did out of hurt, neglect, and emotional damage were about to consume my children and me. What I didn't know was that I was about to get a clear understanding of how my mother felt over the years.

All five of us struggled to find out what a mother's love feels like. We did many things to ourselves and dragged our kids and spouses into our world of dysfunction. Only one person had the answer to why. Her reasons for her lack of love went untold until one day.

In February 2012, I got my answer while driving my mother from North Carolina to Indiana to visit my sick sister. I will never forget what my mother told me in conversation or her tone.

A conversation that took place in the car

It went like this: (discussing my sister)

Me: "We need you as a mother."

Mom: "No, you don't; y'all turned out alright."

Me: "We are not alright; we needed you to love us. Your daughter is sick, and she needs your love."

Mom: "Hell, I never loved any of you."

Me: "All five of us?"

Mom: "Yep."

(thirty seconds of silence)

Me: "Don't you know God wakes you up every day to give you a chance to change your relationships? Don't you want to fix them?"

Mom: "Nope."

There was silence for the next two hours in the car. I was ready, but I was not ready. I was ready because I knew a year prior that I had to change my life to make sure my children would not go through what I went through. I was not ready to hear my mother bluntly say our projection of love towards her all those years meant nothing. I could only thank God that I had been delivered before receiving this revelation. The confession I heard from my mother shed light on events I could not quite understand from my childhood. I was able to connect the dots. I was not angry because it was a confirmation that I was on the right path of thinking—the path of giving up the search for something I had not found when I didn't even know what I was seeking.

WHAT NEEDS TO CHANGE?

We cannot change our past, nor can we fix our parents. Many things have gone wrong in the evolution of the family. We have embraced our current state of dysfunction as the norm. The cycle is passed down from generation to generation. What happens is that many of the children do not have the answers to why the family has become dysfunctional. No one wants to openly tell the truth and point the finger at an elder or a parent. Some will fight change because the dysfunctional lifestyle has been adapted and they see no need for change.

Case in point: families living in the projects or low-income housing. A family may have three or four generations living in the same complex. The next generation's foundation comes from the teachings and practices of the previous generation. As new parents and adults, we must make overt efforts to create a new history for our families. Will this cause a divide in some families? I have to say yes because those who have embraced this way of life will resist change.

The lack of fathers in homes is an issue. Mothers are forced to fill in for the absence of fathers. Grandparents were being forced to step into the roles of the cardinal parents. Young parents are silently hurting from events from their childhood and are building their foundation on dysfunctional information. We must establish a new foundation for our children by sharing the truth of our family orientation, no matter how grim it may seem, to understand what needs to be corrected or removed.

YOUR TOMORROW

I see the same look in the eyes of many of the children today. My story may not be your story, and your pain may not be the same. We all want and need to be held, cared for, and loved. It is instinctive to yearn for those things from our parents. I'm not going to tell you that you will get the same answer I did. I must say that if your parents don't love you as they should, you must learn to love yourself to stop the cycle of dysfunction. My children do not have emotional connections to my past. It is my job to ensure that they are loved, hugged, and treated like family. I know that you have this burning question in your head: "What about me?" You must do what I did; I became my own dad. I had to think about my children's children and their children. No one but you is going to stop family dysfunction. That is going to require you to make children greater than yourself. Create your own field of love that will yield a wealth of

Preface

52

BONUS BOOK 2

WHEN YOU WAKE UP

Let The Healing Begin

TABLE OF CONTENTS

PREFACE

We spend a good portion of our lives doing what we want to do, loving who we want to love, and leaving them at the drop of a hat. We take pride in being rebellious about the things we didn't like about our upbringing. We have quit jobs, crushed our credit, and had some children. There is a price for doing what we want, but we are often not prepared to pay the piper. I feel that if everyone lived their life like that, we would have a huge mess on our hands. As I look at people today, this is what is happening. Even worse, the thought of how we are going to change this trend we have created is staggering. One day you are going to wake up and decide you must put your life in order. That is what happened to me. I woke up to a mess, and I had to move forward in my life or forever hide in my house. No one wins when Dad hides in the house.

THE MESS I MADE

The best way to start this off is with a promise to keep this real and 100% to the very last word. I cannot ask people to consider their hearts for change if I'm not willing to be honest with myself and my readers. When a man is unloved and untrained before he leaves the nest, he will make a mess of his life and ultimately the lives of those in his charge. If he does not wake up and learn his role, he can cause generations of pain and dysfunction for his children. The word that was often used to describe me by a lifelong friend was arrogant. That arrogance stemmed from a false sense of confidence in my abilities as a man. I did not know my personal power, and for a good portion of my life, I did not know where to get it.

Let me start with where I went wrong in love. I did not know what love was, where it came from, or how it was to be displayed. To the untrained man, it meant sex; the more sex you had, the more love you displayed. I searched for sex until I had more children than my check could handle. As the years went by, I started to get a clue, but by that time I had created pockets full of Poseys (pun intended). It was my goal to meet my need for love through my children. I was thoroughly wrong, and in turn, I hurt some of my children through my absence. I was just like the father I am trying to redirect today. I had no right to make a child because I was looking to fill a missing piece in me. I had no right to take a wife without knowing what love was. I was going through the motions as I saw fit as an adult male. When you are an adult male moving about the planet, you can do a lot of covert damage to a lot of people. However, I cannot undo what has been done to my children or me. I am responsible for what I have done and for who I have hurt in my path. I lived with the shame of my choices for years, and no one can say anything worse to me than what I have said in the mirror time and time again to wake myself up.

NO ONE TO BLAME

Family dysfunction breeds a whole basketful of issues not often seen by the naked eye and yet to be revealed. I think it is safe to say that most of us know that when a son lacks a connection to his mother and a daughter lacks a connection to her father, there is a good chance for emotional damage, which can lead to many relationship failures. In my case, there was a disconnection between both, and I had no clue how it was going to affect me. Even worse, I didn't know how I needed to fix my life until it was a mess. We can see families on the streets, in restaurants, while we are at church, and in the malls. You cannot always see dysfunction as if it were a t-shirt with a big "D" on it. No one could see my mess because I was a water-walking Marine. I can't say I tried to hide my dysfunctional ways; I just couldn't see them because that was my norm. I couldn't afford to slow down to see what effect I had on those I married or fathered.

Once you take on a man's role by creating a life, placing blame on someone else is not an option. The differences between adult males and grown men lie in their understanding of two things. #1: Be responsible for the choices you make in life. #2: Hold yourself accountable before anyone else for those choices you made. A grown man will not seek to blame anyone else for his decisions.

LIVE WITHOUT EXCUSES

When I turned forty-five, I had run out of excuses not to move forward in my personal life. By this period of my life, I had clearly understood my role in the decisions I had made over the years. There was no going back in time and undoing any choice I had made. I created my today, which would ultimately become my children's tomorrow. I came to the realization that I needed to repair the paths I created from my misinformation or lack of understanding of what love is. I must make better decisions from this day forward until the end of my life. I will also have to model accountability and responsibility for my children. Excuses are the tools of the lazy, and lazy parents raise lazy children. If I am to leave a legacy of strong and capable citizens, then it must start with me.

"It is sad when excuses govern a man's life. He shall be exposed to his peers as immature and untrustworthy." N2P

SELF-REPAIR

I was not big on self-help books; I had not been in church for years. However, I wanted and needed a change in myself, and I craved it. I had an idea of the man I wanted to be. He would have the following traits:

- Honest to a fault

- Honorable in actions

- Extremely positive

- Understanding and being open to others

- That guy you want as a friend

Yes, that was a tall order. I took on the task of reinventing myself like my life depended on it. I saw these traits in other people—a little here and a little there—but it was hard to find one who had more than three of the things I listed. So I decided I would fake it until I made it. Before every decision I made, I would ask myself, What would that guy do in this situation?

I practiced the art of taking a breath before I made a choice. Yes, it sounds simple, but we are programmed so deeply into who we are as adults that we have a preset core to our decision-making. Most often, a person's core says pleasure or money first. If that has been the case for years, then it will be hard to change it. They would follow that train of thought for years. When your moral compass just spins because your foundation has not been set, this is the result. Needless to say, you take everyone in your life along for the ride as well.

For eight months, I second-guessed my decision-making. There were things I really enjoyed about the old me. I would fight in bars, and I drank like my mother from time to time. I was selfish about caring for others, and I carried an amount of anger that would make King Kong take a few steps back. My personal goals were above all else. These were things in me that the ones I loved did not see in me.

My inadequate life was easy to hide; at this time in my life, my wife could not and would not live with me. According to her, I was a man of stone. Nothing seemed to bother me. I knew if I wanted people to love me, I would have to put effort into changing that. So I did it; I pretended to be a good man until it was automatic.

"Contrary to what many people think, your brain works for you; you don't work for your brain." N2P

FIX WHAT YOU BROKE

I often see on television where people have offended or done something horrible to another person or group of people. Everyone cries out for an apology of some sort. I believe most apologies are an epic fail. Because most of the offenses carried out against the victims were not by accident. Quite often, it took some thought, planning, and a hint of skill to do what had been done. The apologies that are often given do not make sense to me. The apology does not make the person whole or make the situation better. If you decide to cut down your neighbor's tree because it blocks your view of the lake, you cannot uncut that tree. There is no undoing that; therefore, your apology is useless. If you replace the tree with something to the liking of your neighbor, then you can apologize. In our early years of life, we make a lot of emotional decisions, and they cannot be undone.

It is my goal in life to attempt to make anyone I have emotionally harmed whole because I do not want what happened to me to happen to them. We must unselfishly look at what we have done in our lives to get to this point. Dysfunction says, "Wish it all away, and everyone will be alright," but we know this is not true.

Before writing this book, each time I had a discussion with a friend or co-worker, they shared a piece of their family dysfunction. We have become a society that accepts family dysfunction as the norm, and we seem to be okay with handing it down to the next generation. They ask, "Who's my dad? Why hasn't he come to see me?" They have many other unanswered questions. We must swallow our shame, wipe the tears from our faces, and listen to the almost silent cries of those who did not ask to come into this world. We too must stand ready to be rejected. It is often said, "It is never too late to change." I remember when I was so mad at my mother and father that I didn't even want them to change. But deep inside, I really did need them to change. I needed them to change to break the cycle of dysfunction they were in and make it better for me.

THE PLEA

There needs to come a time in our lives when the needs of our children truly come first. The years of passing down old, outdated pain to generations to come must stop. When we look at the world and the children of today, we can see we are at our breaking point. If you care about where we are going as a people, let this be your wake-up call. First, you must change yourself to change the child. If you change the child, you will change the world. When you look at the level of pain and self-hate, you will see that selfishness and old pain worked like a charm to make the unloved children of today.

Never Ending

Please read my other Book

"Batteries and Suckers"

MEET THE AUTHOR

There are many layers to being a man; there's the one we think we know, and then there is the one that is buried under a pile of bad decisions and old pain. When he wakes up, he has to make a choice, not only for himself but for those who look to him for leadership and guidance. I challenge every capable man to find his way to greatness because our children need us.

Paul **"Kacky"** Posey

www.ingramcontent.com/pod-product-compliance
Lightning Source LLC
Chambersburg PA
CBHW011240120626
46549CB00009B/3350